How Ella Discovered Her Superpowers with Yoga

A gentle giant elephant named Ella lived in the heart of the jungle. She spent her days wandering the lush forests, enjoying the beauty of nature. Ellie loved to go on adventures with her friends.

As much as Ella loved to play with her friends, she struggled to keep up with them on their adventures. Sometimes Ella felt too slow or that she needed to be stronger. Ella became very sad. So Ella went to find one of her closest friends, the wise owl of the forest, Luna.

She told Luna how sad she was and wondered how she could become stronger and faster to keep up with all her friends on their adventures.

Finally, Luna explained there was a way to uncover her hidden superpowers. It was a practice called yoga. Luna was perched on a branch and looked down at Ella. “Have you ever heard of yoga?” she asked.

Ella was excited! “No, I haven't. What is it?”

Luna slapped her wings and settled onto a lower branch to talk to Ella. “Yoga is all about stretching and breathing,” she said. “It’s like playing a game with your body. When you do certain poses, you'll start to feel stronger and notice you can do more things with your body. As you practice more, you'll uncover new superpowers you didn't even know you had.”

Ella's eyes widened with excitement. "Really? That sounds amazing! Can you show me how to do yoga?"

"Of course," Luna said. "Let's start with a simple pose called butterfly. Sit down on the ground and bring the bottoms of your feet together, flap your knees up and down like butterfly wings. Don't forget to take deep breaths in through the nose and out through the mouth while doing it."

So Ella sat down and tried the pose. She felt a gentle stretch of her legs. She breathed in and out as Luna had said, and suddenly she felt a warmness spread throughout her body.

Ella told Luna, “Wow, that felt amazing!” After that, Ella felt like she could take longer steps, allowing her to move faster.

Luna smiled. “That's the magic of yoga. With every pose you do, you'll uncover new powers and feel more connected to your body and the world around you.”

Ella was eager to try out this magical yoga even more. She wanted to feel stronger and happier, as Luna promised. So Luna showed her how to do tree pose.

First, Ella stood tall like a tree, planting her feet firmly on the ground. Then, she raised one leg and bent it, placing her foot on the opposite thigh, like a branch growing from the trunk of a tree, breathing in through her trunk and out through her mouth like Luna had told her to do.

Luna explained that the tree pose helped animals feel strong and grounded, like a tree with deep roots. Ella imagined herself as a tall and sturdy tree, swaying gently in the breeze, and she felt a new sense of strength and confidence.

Ella held the pose and felt her body's strength grow like a tree's trunk. She also felt a sense of calm and peace, like the peaceful forest surrounding her.

Ella was amazed by how powerful she felt just by doing a simple pose. She couldn't wait to learn more yoga poses and uncover more superpowers.

Ella found a peaceful spot in the forest, closed her eyes, and started to breathe deeply. She lifted her trunk, stretched her legs, and felt light as a feather and strong.

As she practiced yoga more and more, Ella noticed something interesting. She was becoming stronger, faster, and more powerful than ever before. She could balance on one leg for minutes at a time, and her trunk was more flexible than ever.

Ella was amazed by these changes and wondered if it was her imagination. But she realized it was real when she tried lifting a heavy log with her trunk. She had gained superpowers!

Excited by her new superpowers, Ella played with her powers. She tried different yoga poses, and with each pose, she discovered a new superpower.

As Ella began doing more yoga poses, her body became stronger. Cobra pose was her favorite because it made her feel super-fast, just like a snake!

Luna showed Ella how to do cobra pose by laying down on her belly with her hands underneath her shoulders. Then, she slowly lifted her chest off the ground, like a snake raising its head to look around.

Ella tried the cobra pose, lifted her chest off the ground as she inhaled, and lowered her chest back to the ground as she exhaled. She felt her muscles grow stronger. She imagined herself slithering through the jungle fast as a snake, which excited her!

She was amazed by how much she had changed since practicing yoga. She was stronger and faster than ever before. She knew it was all because of yoga.

With her newfound superpowers, Ella felt like she could conquer anything and keep up with her friends through all their adventures.

Yoga had become Ella's favorite way to explore her body and mind. She was so grateful to Luna!

Ella decided to share what she had learned with all her friends in the jungle.

She gathered friends from the forest and began teaching her friends how to find their own superpowers. Soon more animals were curious to join her.

Ella taught them the different poses of yoga, like tree, cobra, and more, showing them how to stretch, breathe and move. They practiced different poses and discovered their special superpowers.

The giraffe discovered she could stretch her neck even further, and the monkey found he could climb higher. The snake found she could move faster than ever, and the zebra discovered he could run incredibly fast.

As more animals discovered their superpowers through yoga, they started to enjoy the practice. So they formed a yoga group in the jungle, practicing together daily and helping each other grow stronger.

Ella was proud of what she had accomplished. She had found her superpowers and helped other animals discover theirs.

The animals in the jungle became happier, healthier, and stronger. They felt more connected to nature and each other.

Ella could keep up with all her friends on their adventures. She had discovered that yoga could give her superpowers, and her life was changed. She felt grateful to live with such wonderful friends and could now enjoy their adventures together.

All the animals were so happy that Ella had helped them find their superpowers, and they threw Ella a big jungle party.

Made in the USA
Las Vegas, NV
16 July 2023